GE AND THANK THE FOLLOWIN

NTED PERMISSION FOR THE F

EFFORTS HAVE BEEN MADE

WE APOLOGISE TO ANY THAT WE HAVE

NER (THAMES ROAD BRIDGE); DYFFRYN

N SEASIDE ESTATE); E T W DENNIS AND

HOPPING CENTRE, TOWNGATE, LEYLAND;

SONS LTD (CAISTER CHALET, CAISTER

CAMP, HAYLING ISLAND, HAMPSHIRE);

CENTRAL LIBRARY, ST NICHOLAS WAY,

OF CHATHAM PRINTERS LTD, LEICESTER,

SALE); JOAN MACRAE (A40 TRAFFIC);

RREG GOCH CARAVAN PARK, MORFA

FORTE'S RESTAURANT

ON THE M.1.

THE M.I. MOTORWAY.
Fifty Five Miles in Length,
it is spanned by 134 bridges.

BLUE STAR

APPROACH TO THE SERVICE AREA

PEDESTRIAN BRIDGE OVER THE M.1.

NUL.36F. M.6. Motorway. Newcastle-under-Lyme.

KBH.33F. The Motorway. Knebworth.

NUL.30F. M.6. Motorway. Newcastle-under-Lyme.

ET.1668

M.6 MOTORWAY

Fortes, M.6 Motorway, Charnock Richard. ET.405

The M1 near Newport Pagnell.

FRITH
NPG 58

AERIAL VIEW OF THE SERVICE AREA ON THE M.5.

BRIDGE AND RESTAURANT ON THE A.1. NORTH OF DONCASTER M 6433

Always a Welcome at Fortes, M.6 Motorway, Keele, Staffs. ET.2941

LONDON · The Grill Room, Fortes Scratchwood Service Area, M1 Motorway ET5724

Fortes Corley Service Area. M6 Motorway (Midlands Link) OF 28

Fortes Corley Service Area. M6 Motorway (Midlands Link)

Fortes, M.6 Motorway, Charnock Richard.

ET.3740

Forton service area, M6 Motorway

CWB.82. THE BYPASS, COWBRIDGE.

MERSEY TUNNEL JUNCTION CHAMBER, SHOWING MAIN AND BRANCH TUNNEL G-1131

INTERIOR OF MERSEY TUNNEL, LIVERPOOL G. 270

A 40 TRAFFIC Photo. by Mrs. J. MacRae, Cassington W.I.

THAMES ROAD BRIDGE

PTH.41. Amlwch Road. Pentraeth.

NUL.42F. Town Centre By-Pass. Newcastle under Lyme.

The Cross, Kingswinford, Staffs.

The Drive In Bottle Shop, Northampton

CYN.170. The Underpass. Croydon.

QUEENSWAY, BIRMINGHAM

The Bull Ring, Birmingham

Smallbrook Ringway, Birmingham

Croydon Centre

The Bus Station, Ashton-Under-Lyne

Bus Station, Exeter

Bus Station and Shopping Centre, Hanley

The New Bus Station, Preston (Largest in Britain).

P.2423

BUS STATION, HALIFAX

TONYPANDY CAR PARK AND TREALAW

Drayton Parslow Centre

Harlow New Town

TOWN CENTRE REDDITCH. TRAFFIC INTERCHANGE

TOLWORTH TOWER

EFY.4 PROSPECT RING, EAST FINCHLEY COPYRIGHT
FRITH LTD

Towyn, Foryd Road

The Street, Rustington.

ET.1687

The Subway, Oldham.

3

High Street, Frimley

F.2301

The Leisure Centre, Sale

– KNBT 4477

Wulfrun Centre, Wolverhampton

W.0504

Market Square, Burnley

B.8802L

New Shopping Centre, Preston

Town Centre, Stevenage

S.7103L

Mersey Shopping Precinct, Stockport

C.2908

THE PRECINCT, COVENTRY

GWENT SQUARE, CWMBRAN

New Shopping Centre, Burton on Trent

B.6805

Queen's Square, Crawley.

ET.1232

New Shopping Centre, Towngate, Leyland. 1

Carlton Court, Westbury

Market Precinct, Scunthorpe

S.0803L

The Butts Shopping Centre, Reading

FARNHAM

POST OFFICE

Mural by Michael Fairclough incorporating in abstract form landscape features surrounding Farnham: Alice Holt, Crooksbury Hill, Characteristic shapes and textures of the fields to the West of the town. The town itself is represented by two barlike shapes of red brick.

Basingstoke

BASILDON

THE MARTLETS

QUEENS SQUARE

THE SHOPPING CENTRE, CRAWLEY

QUEENS SQUARE & QUEENSWAY

THE BOULEVARD

THE TOWN HALL, ROMFORD

Brent Cross Shopping Centre, London

The Mall, Arndale Centre, Crossgates

The Frenchgate Centre, Doncaster

D.1715L

Quadrant Arcade, Swansea

S.2550

County Hall and Town Centre, Barnsley

B.0402

Civic Centre, Plymouth

P.0859

The New Swimming Baths, Crosby

W.4308

New Swimming Baths, Coventry

The Lochgelly Centre Complex

5839

The Library, Luton

The Library, Corby

FRITH
CBY 62

Central Library, St. Nicholas Way, Sutton

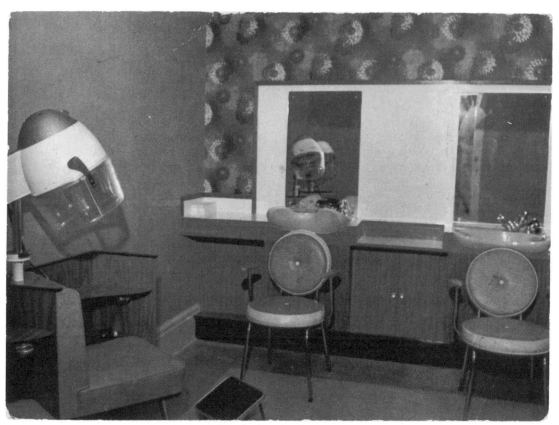

London Transport Benevolent Fund Home at Hythe, near Folkstone

Canteen, Stoke Mandeville Hospital

Hearts of Oak Benefit Society, Convalescent Home, Broadstairs

P/AGR 44 CHESHIRE COLLEGE OF EDUCATION ALSAGER *Premisc*

MIRFIELD MODERN SCHOOL

Watfield College of Technology, Hatfield

Churchill College, Cambridge

CYN. 143. CROYDON TECHNICAL COLLEGE
THE DENNING HALL.

New Technical College, Blackburn

B.7216

Denman College, The Library

Transport & General Workers' Union Recuperation Centre, Littleport

BDA.102F. AUSTIN TAYLOR FACTORY, BETHESDA.

AERIAL VIEW OF REDDITCH NEW TOWN. WASHFORD INDUSTRIAL AREA

National Giro Centre, Bootle

B.9705

Thomas Cook International Headquarters

PTL.13 The Nylon Factory, Pontypool.

STP 13 Jansel House, Stopsley

New Head Office, Pilkington Brothers Limited, St Helens

KEMNAY QUARRIES

P/EP 101F THE SHELL REFINERY, ELLESMERE PORT

Promise

CEGB Didcot Power Station, Oxfordshire

Turbine Hall, CEGB Wylfa Nuclear Power Station, Anglesey

Hinkley Point Nuclear Power Station, Somerset

Hunterston 'B' Nuclear Power Station, Ayrshire

Sizewell Nuclear Power Station, Leiston

THE FAST REACTOR, DOUNREAY, CAITHNESS 52/162

LONDON · Luton Airport

05731

Control Tower, Luton Airport

Lounge Manchester Airport

M.002109L

London Airport Control Tower

LONDON · *Terminal 2, Heathrow Airport, London.* ET5703

Stansted Airport · London

New Terminal Building, Glamorgan (Rhoose) Airport. 123

Terminal Buildings, Glasgow Airport, Scotland.

AT.1788R

Manchester Airport Hotel, The Excelsior.

ET.4385

The Lansdowne Court Hotel, Belfast

A corner of the Moota Motel, Cockermouth

The Fortes Excelsior Motor Lodge, nr. Pontefract, Yorkshire. 5672XR

The Foyer, Ocean Hotel, Sandown, Isle of Wight

Izaak Walton Hotel, Dovedale

The Lounge Bar, Devon Coast Country Club, Paignton

CAVENDISH HOTEL

POLICE NOTICE
NO PARKING

Raleigh's Wall, Budleigh Salterton

B.2939

Sandhead from the South

Waterloo

KN 1194

Southerness Shopping Centre

LOOKING ACROSS SOLWAY FIRTH, SILLOTH

ROSE GARDEN, SILLOTH

Freshwater Caravan Camp, Burton Bradstock

OUR CARAVAN

Reighton Sands Holiday Village F.0287

GTE.9. CROWSNEST CARAVAN CAMP FROM THE CLIFFS, GRISTHORPE.

South End Caravan Park, Walney Island

P/DFN 130 DYFFRYN SEASIDE ESTATE

Promise

P/27 A GARREG GOCH CARAVAN PARK, MORFA BYCHAN *Promise*

Ty Mawr Holiday Park

8028

Holywell Bay Caravan Park

LWG.49F. The Chalets. Llandanwg.

BC 38 The Chalets, Cherry Farm Caravan Park, Burgh Castle.

Sunshine Holiday Camp, Hayling Island, Hampshire

Caister Chalet, Caister Holiday Camp

New Chalets, Golden Sands Holiday Camp, Hopton-on-Sea. ET.1765

Pontins Holiday Village, Camber Sands

THE SLEEPING BLOCKS, WEMBURY POINT HOLIDAY CAMP.

THE GLADE. HOLIDAY CAMP. CORTON.

SUN LOUNGE, BUTLIN'S, BOGNOR REGIS BR 3

BUTLIN'S BOGNOR REGIS
The Reception Hall

BUTLIN'S CLACTON
Typical Dining Hall

BUTLIN'S SKEGNESS
A CORNER OF THE GARDEN

The Swimming Pool, Trevose Golf and Country Club.

The Golf Club, Appleby.

APY 45

MONKS' REST TEA GARDENS, WORLEBURY, WESTON-SUPER-MARE

VIEW FROM THE
BERRY COURT HOLIDAY FLATLETS,
BRIXHAM, SOUTH DEVON

Tom Long's Post, Minchinhampton Common

The Tourist Information Centre, Fort William

VIEWS AROUND HASLINGDEN

MALPAS COURT ESTATE, NEWPORT

W 7260

Drawing Room, "Westerley", Minehead

Photo. H. A. Summers, Minehead

Bridle Road, Eastham 26664

BIRK DALE, LITTLE COMMON D19446

14.9 ELMSALL HILL, SOUTH ELMSALL.

Main Road, Kelsale PN597

Pleasantly situated split-level houses in Cumberland

HIGHFIELD FLATS—HALESOWEN

Kirkland Hill Peterlee.

ERITH
PDE 18

West Road, Crook.

Mulberry Close, North Thoresby. NT 10

STN 52 St. Paul's Drive, Syston.

A BEND ON PORLOCK HILL

RAIN CLOUDS, FROM SOUTHEND PIER. 2053.

COLLECTION MARTIN PARR